Bible
Promises
for My
Teacher

**BROADMAN
& HOLMAN
PUBLISHERS**

Nashville, Tennessee

Contents

Promises to Start your Day

Each new day promises . . . what? More than you can handle? Enough work for three people? Papers to grade? Lesson plans to organize?

If you knew that today promised the reality of God's presence, would it make a difference? If you knew that something meaningful and eternal was going to occur in the next twenty-four hours, would you stand a better chance of seeing it when it happens? If you knew that the Lord had already measured out your workload— and equipped you with the strength to match— would your day start looking up?

The Sunrise of Worship

May You Be My First Thought of the Day

I will sing of Your strength
  and will joyfully proclaim
  Your faithful love in the morning.
For You have been a stronghold for me,
  a refuge in my day of trouble.
To You, my strength, I sing praises,
  because God is my stronghold—
  my faithful God.

Psalm 59:16-17

Wake up, my soul!
   Wake up, harp and lyre!
   I will wake up the dawn.
I will praise You, Lord, among the peoples;
   I will sing praises to You among the nations.
For Your faithful love is as high as the heavens;
   Your faithfulness reaches to the clouds.
God, be exalted above the heavens;
   let Your glory be over the whole earth.

Psalm 57:8-11

You crown the year with Your goodness;
   Your ways overflow with plenty.
The wilderness pastures overflow,
   and the hills are robed with joy.
The pastures are clothed with flocks,
   and the valleys covered with grain.
They shout in triumph; indeed, they sing.

Psalm 65:11-13

From the rising of the sun to its setting,
   let the name of the LORD be praised.

Psalm 113:3

It is good to praise the LORD,
  to sing praise to Your name, Most High,
  to declare Your faithful love in the morning
  and Your faithfulness at night.

Psalm 92:1-2

Better a day in Your courts
  than a thousand anywhere else.
I would rather be at the door
  of the house of my God
  than to live in the tents of the wicked.
For the LORD God is a sun and shield.
  The LORD gives grace and glory;
  He does not withhold the good
  from those who live with integrity.
LORD of Hosts,
  happy is the person who trusts in You!

Psalm 84:10-12

Those who know Your name trust in You
  because You have not abandoned
  those who seek You, LORD.

Psalm 9:10

Satisfy us in the morning with Your
faithful love so that we may shout
with joy and be glad all our days.
Make us rejoice for as many days
as You have humbled us,
for as many years as we have seen adversity.
Let Your work be seen by Your servants,
and Your splendor by their children.
Let the favor of the Lord our God be upon us;
establish for us the work of our hands—
establish the work of our hands!

Psalm 90:14-17

*To my early knowledge of the Bible
I owe the best part of my taste in
literature, the most precious and,
on the whole, the one essential
part of my education.*

—John Ruskin

I will praise You every day;
  I will honor Your name forever and ever.
The LORD is great and is highly praised;
  His greatness is unsearchable.
One generation will declare
  Your works to the next
  and will proclaim Your mighty acts.
I will speak of Your glorious splendor
  and Your wonderful works. . . .
All You have made
  will praise You, LORD;
  the godly will bless You.
They will speak of the glory of Your kingdom
  and will declare Your might,
  informing all people of Your mighty acts
  and of the glorious splendor
  of Your kingdom.

Psalm 145:2-5, 10-12

The Sunrise of Worship

My mouth will tell about Your righteousness
   and Your salvation all day long,
      though I cannot sum them up.

Psalm 71:15

I will praise the LORD at all times;
   His praise will always be on my lips.
I will boast in the LORD;
   the humble will hear and be glad.

Psalm 34:1-2

Sing to the LORD,
   for He has done glorious things.
   Let this be known throughout the earth.
Cry out and sing, citizen of Zion,
   for the Holy One of Israel is among you.

Isaiah 12:5-6a

Let them give thanks to the LORD
   for His faithful love and
   His wonderful works for the human race.
For He has satisfied the thirsty
   and filled the hungry with good things.

Psalm 107:8-9

The Surrender of Prayer

I Start This Day Dependent on You

At daybreak, LORD, You hear my voice;
  at daybreak I plead my case to You
  and watch expectantly. . . .
I enter Your house by the abundance
  of Your faithful love;
  I bow down toward Your holy temple
  in reverential awe of You.

Psalm 5:3, 7

I call to You for help, LORD;
   in the morning my prayer meets You.

Psalm 88:13

I call with all my heart; answer me, LORD.
   I will obey Your statutes.
I call to You; save me,
   and I will keep Your decrees.
I rise before dawn and cry out for help;
   I hope in Your word.
I am awake through each watch of the night
   to meditate on Your promise.

Psalm 119:145-148

Let me experience Your faithful love
   in the morning, for I trust in You.
Reveal to me the way I should go,
   because I long for You.
Rescue me from my enemies, LORD;
   I come to You for protection.
Teach me to do Your will, for You are my God.
   May Your gracious Spirit
   lead me on level ground.

Psalm 143:8-10

When, on my bed, I think of You,
  I meditate on You during the night watches
  because You are my help;
  I will rejoice in the shadow of Your wings.
I follow close to You;
  Your right hand holds on to me.

Psalm 63:6-8

Even before they call, I will answer;
  while they are still speaking, I will hear.

Isaiah 65:24

The LORD is near all who call out to Him,
  all who call out to Him with integrity.
He fulfills the desires of those who fear Him;
  He hears their cry for help and saves them.

Psalm 145:18-19

Now this is the confidence we have before
Him: whenever we ask anything according to
His will, He hears us. And if we know that He
hears whatever we ask, we know that we have
what we have asked Him for.

1 John 5:14-15

The Surrender of Prayer

In the same way the Spirit also joins to help in our weakness, because we do not know what to pray for as we should, but the Spirit Himself intercedes for us with unspoken groanings.

And He who searches the hearts knows the Spirit's mind-set, because He intercedes for the saints according to the will of God.

Romans 8:26-27

Keep asking, and it will be given to you. Keep searching, and you will find. Keep knocking, and the door will be opened to you.

Matthew 7:7

We become aware that our task is not so much to master the text of Scripture as to be mastered by the Source of that text.

–Marjorie Thompson

How lovely is Your dwelling place,
   LORD of Hosts.
My soul longs, even languishes,
   for the courts of the LORD;
   my heart and flesh cry out
   for the living God.
Even a sparrow finds a home,
   and a swallow, a nest for herself
   where she places her young—
   near Your altars, LORD of Hosts,
   my King and my God. . . .
Happy are the people
   whose strength is in You,
   whose hearts are set on pilgrimage.
As they pass through the Valley of Baca,
   they make it a source of springwater;
   even the autumn rain
   will cover it with blessings.
They go from strength to strength.

Psalm 84:1-3, 5-7a

The Surrender of Prayer

Be gracious to me, Lord,
   for I call to You all day long.
Bring joy to Your servant's life,
   since I set my hope on You, Lord.
For You, Lord, are kind and ready to forgive,
   abundant in faithful love
   to all who call on You.

Psalm 86:3-5

Therefore since we have a great high priest
who has passed through the heavens—Jesus the
Son of God—let us hold fast to the confession.
For we do not have a high priest who is unable
to sympathize with our weaknesses, but One
who has been tested in every way as we are,
yet without sin.

   Therefore let us approach the throne of grace
with boldness, so that we may receive mercy
and find grace to help us at the proper time.

Hebrews 4:14-16

I will wait for the God who saves me.
   My God will hear me.

Micah 7:7b

The Value of Discipline

Help Me Learn the Beauty of Obedience

Depart from evil and do good,
  and dwell there forever.
For the LORD loves justice
  and will not abandon His faithful ones.
They are kept safe forever.

Psalm 37:27-28a

How can I repay the LORD
   all the good He has done for me?
I will take the cup of salvation
   and worship the LORD.
I will fulfill my vows to the LORD
   in the presence of all His people.

Psalm 116:12-14

For the LORD gives wisdom;
   from His mouth come
   knowledge and understanding.
He stores up success for the upright;
   He is a shield for those
   who live with integrity
   so that He may guard the paths of justice
   and protect the way of His loyal followers.

Proverbs 2:6-8

How great is Your goodness
   that You have stored up
   for those who fear You,
   and accomplished in the sight of everyone
   for those who take refuge in You.

Psalm 31:19

Love the LORD, all His faithful ones.
    The LORD protects the loyal,
    but fully repays the arrogant.
Be strong and courageous,
    all you who hope in the LORD.

Psalm 31:23-24

You who love the LORD, hate evil!
    He protects the lives of His godly ones;
    He rescues them from the
    hand of the wicked.
Light dawns for the righteous,
    gladness for the upright in heart.
Be glad in the LORD, you righteous ones,
    and praise His holy name.

Psalm 97:10-12

If anyone wants to come with Me, he must
deny himself, take up his cross daily, and follow Me. For whoever wants to save his life will
lose it, but whoever loses his life because of
Me will save it.

Luke 9:23-24

The Value of Discipline

Do you not know that the runners in a stadium all race, but only one receives the prize? Run in such a way that you may win.

Now everyone who competes exercises self-control in everything. However, they do it to receive a perishable crown, but we an imperishable one. Therefore I do not run like one who runs aimlessly, or box like one who beats the air. Instead, I discipline my body and bring it under strict control, so that after preaching to others, I myself will not be disqualified.

1 Corinthians 9:24-27

The study of God's Word, for the purpose of discovering God's will, is the secret discipline which has formed the greatest characters.

—J. W. Alexander

God—His way is perfect;
   the word of the LORD is pure.
He is a shield to all
   who take refuge in Him.
For who is God besides the LORD?
   And who is a rock? Only our God.
God—He clothes me with strength
   and makes my way perfect.
He makes my feet like the feet of a deer
   and sets me securely on the heights.
He trains my hands for war;
   my arms can bend a bow of bronze.
You have given me the shield of Your salvation;
   Your right hand upholds me,
   and Your humility exalts me.
You widen a place beneath me for my steps,
   and my ankles do not give way.

Psalm 18:30-36

The Value of Discipline

Who then is a faithful and sensible slave, whom his master has put in charge of his household, to give them food at the proper time? Blessed is that slave whom his master, when he comes, will find working. I assure you: He will put him in charge of all his possessions.

Matthew 24:45-47

Therefore, get your minds ready for action, being self-disciplined, and set your hope completely on the grace to be brought to you at the revelation of Jesus Christ.

As obedient children, do not be conformed to the desires of your former ignorance but, as the One who called you is holy, you also are to be holy in all your conduct; for it is written, "Be holy, because I am holy."

1 Peter 1:13-16

For if you live according to the flesh, you are going to die. But if by the Spirit you put to death the deeds of the body, you will live.

Romans 8:13

The Gift of Grace

Thank You, Lord, for Being So Merciful

May our Lord Jesus Christ Himself and God our Father, who has loved us and given us eternal encouragement and good hope by grace, encourage your hearts and strengthen you in every good work and word.

2 Thessalonians 2:16-17

Blessed be the God and Father of our Lord Jesus Christ. According to His great mercy, He has given us a new birth into a living hope through the resurrection of Jesus Christ from the dead, and into an inheritance that is imperishable, uncorrupted, and unfading, kept in heaven for you, who are being protected by God's power through faith for a salvation that is ready to be revealed in the last time.

You rejoice in this, though now for a short time you have had to be distressed by various trials so that the genuineness of your faith—more valuable than gold, which perishes though refined by fire—may result in praise, glory, and honor at the revelation of Jesus Christ.

1 Peter 1:3-7

By God's grace I am what I am.

1 Corinthians 15:10a

For we have all received
grace after grace from His fullness.

John 1:16

For you know the grace of our Lord Jesus Christ: although He was rich, for your sake He became poor, so that by His poverty you might become rich.

2 Corinthians 8:9

For God did not send His Son into the world that He might judge the world, but that the world might be saved through Him.

John 3:17

But when the goodness and love for man
appeared from God our Savior,
He saved us—not by works
of righteousness that we had done,
but according to His mercy,
through the washing of regeneration
and renewal by the Holy Spirit.
This Spirit He poured out on us abundantly
through Jesus Christ our Savior,
so that having been justified by His grace,
we may become heirs with
the hope of eternal life.

Titus 3:4-7

The Gift of Grace

Now everything is from God, who reconciled us to Himself through Christ and gave us the ministry of reconciliation: that is, in Christ, God was reconciling the world to Himself, not counting their trespasses against them, and He has committed the message of reconciliation to us. . . . He made the One who did not know sin to be sin for us, so that we might become the righteousness of God in Him.

2 Corinthians 5:18-19, 21

The Bible is a book in comparison with which all others in my eyes are of minor importance; and which in all my perplexities and distresses has never failed to give me light and strength.

—Robert E. Lee

If the LORD had not been on our side—
  let Israel say—
If the LORD had not been on our side
  when men attacked us, then they
  would have swallowed us alive
  in their burning anger against us.
Then the waters would have engulfed us;
  the torrent would have swept over us;
  the raging waters would have swept over us.
Praise the LORD,
  who has not let us
  be ripped apart by their teeth.
We have escaped like a bird
  from the hunter's net;
  the net is torn, and we have escaped.
Our help is in the name of the LORD,
  the Maker of heaven and earth.

Psalm 124:1-8

The Gift of Grace

May you be strengthened with all
power, according to His glorious might,
for all endurance and patience, with joy giving
thanks to the Father, who has enabled you to
share in the saints' inheritance in the light.

Colossians 1:11-12

For by grace you are saved through faith, and
this is not from yourselves; it is God's gift—
not from works, so that no one can boast. For
we are His creation—created in Christ Jesus
for good works, which God prepared ahead of
time so that we should walk in them.

Ephesians 2:8-10

He called you to this through our gospel, so
that you might obtain the glory of our Lord
Jesus Christ.

2 Thessalonians 2:14

This is the true grace of God.
Take your stand in it!

1 Peter 5:12b

The Hope of New Beginnings

Today Could Be the Start of . . . What?

"For I know the plans I have for you," says the LORD, "wholesome plans and not harmful, to give you a future and hope.

"You will call to Me and come and pray to Me. Then I will listen to you. You will seek Me and find Me if you seek for Me with all your heart."

Jeremiah 29:11-13

Restore us to Yourself, O LORD,
that we may return;
renew our days as in former times.

Lamentations 5:21

You have a mighty arm;
Your hand is powerful;
Your right hand is lifted high. . . .
Happy are the people
who know the joyful shout;
LORD, they walk in the light
of Your presence.
They rejoice in Your name all day long,
and they are exalted by Your righteousness.
For You are their magnificent strength.

Psalm 89:13, 15-17a

Are there any among the nothings
of the nations that can bring rain?
Or can the skies alone give showers?
Are You not the One, O LORD, our God?
We therefore put our hope in You,
for You have done all these things.

Jeremiah 14:22

The path of the righteous
   is like the light of dawn,
     shining brighter and brighter until midday.

Proverbs 4:18

If you earnestly seek God
   and direct your plea for grace
   to the Almighty,
   if you are pure and upright,
   He will arouse Himself
   even now on your behalf
   and restore the home
   where righteousness lives.
Your beginning was small,
   but your final days
   will be full of prosperity.

Job 8:5-7

Therefore, this is what the LORD says: "If you return, I will restore you; you will stand in My presence. And if you speak precious—rather than worthless—words, you will be like My mouth."

Jeremiah 15:19a

The Hope of New Beginnings

You caused me to experience
  many troubles and misfortunes,
  but You will revive me again.
You will bring me up again,
  even from the depths of the earth.
You will increase my honor
  and comfort me once again.

Psalm 71:20-21

"Not by strength or by might, but by My
Spirit," says the LORD of Hosts.

Zechariah 4:6b

After more than sixty years of almost
daily reading of the Bible, I never fail
to find it always new and marvelously
in tune with the changing needs of
every day.

—Cecil B. DeMille

As for you,
   if you have focused your heart,
   spread your hands to Him in prayer. . . .
Then you will lift up
   your face unblemished;
   you will be firmly established
   and need not fear.
For you will forget about trouble;
   you will recall it the same way
   you remember waters
   that have flowed by.
Life will stand brighter than noon.
   It may be dark,
   but it will become like the morning.
You will be confident,
   because there is hope.
You will look carefully about
   and lie down in safety.

Job 11:13, 15-18

The Hope of New Beginnings

This is what the LORD says: "Keep your voice from weeping and your eyes from tears, for the reward for your work will come."

Jeremiah 31:16a

In Him we have redemption through His blood, the forgiveness of our trespasses, according to the riches of His grace that He lavished on us with all wisdom and understanding.

Ephesians 1:7-8

Once you were not a people,
    but now you are God's people;
you had not received mercy,
    but now you have received mercy.

1 Peter 2:10

LORD my God, You have done many things—
    Your wonderful works and Your plans for us;
    none can compare with You.
If I were to report and speak of them,
    they are more than can be told.

Psalm 40:5

Promises
to Get You
Through

From the minute you open the door in the morning, you're center stage. And all day long, you have to think on your feet, stay on your toes, and turn on a dime.

But God will be there to help you keep your balance, to keep the spinning plates in motion. He'll be there to make sure a momentary stumble doesn't bring your whole day down in a crash.

These children need you today. So take your place. Take your stand. Take them one-by-one in your caring hands, and take them one step closer to the future your Father dreams for them.

Helping Them to Persevere

Life Is for the Long Haul

Consider it a great joy, my brothers, whenever you experience various trials, knowing that the testing of your faith produces endurance.

But endurance must do its complete work, so that you may be mature and complete, lacking nothing.

James 1:2-4

I know that all God accomplishes will last forever. Nothing can be added to it, and nothing can be taken away from it. God works so people may stand in awe of Him.

Ecclesiastes 3:14

You, therefore, my child, be strong in the grace that is in Christ Jesus.

2 Timothy 2:1

For if we have died with Him,
   we will also live with Him;
   if we endure, we will also reign with Him.

2 Timothy 2:11b-12a

Affliction produces endurance, endurance produces proven character, and proven character produces hope.

   This hope does not disappoint, because God's love has been poured out in our hearts through the Holy Spirit who was given to us.

Romans 5:3b-5

Promises to Get You Through

Now we ask you, brothers, to give recognition to those who labor among you and lead you in the Lord and admonish you, and to esteem them very highly in love because of their work.

1 Thessalonians 5:12-13a

For the time will come when they will not tolerate sound doctrine, but according to their own desires, will accumulate teachers for themselves because they have an itch to hear something new. They will turn away from hearing the truth and will turn aside to myths. But as for you, keep a clear head about everything, endure hardship.

2 Timothy 4:3-5a

To please the recruiter, no one serving as a soldier gets entangled in the concerns of everyday life. Also, if anyone competes as an athlete, he is not crowned unless he competes according to the rules. It is the hardworking farmer who ought to be the first to get a share of the crops.

2 Timothy 2:4-6

Take the prophets who spoke in the Lord's name as an example of suffering and patience. See, we count as blessed those who have endured. You have heard of Job's endurance and have seen the outcome from the Lord.

James 5:10-11a

The Lord is faithful; He will strengthen and guard you from the evil one.

2 Thessalonians 3:3

Men cannot be well educated without the Bible. It ought, therefore, to hold the chief place in every seat of learning throughout Christendom. I do not know of a higher service that could be rendered to this republic.

—Eliphalett Nott

When you do good and suffer,
   if you endure, it brings favor with God.
For you were called to this,
   because Christ also suffered for you,
   leaving you an example,
   so that you should follow in His steps.
He did not commit sin,
   and no deceit was found in His mouth;
   when reviled, He did not revile in return;
   when suffering, He did not threaten,
   but committed Himself
   to the One who judges justly.
He Himself bore our sins in His body
   on the tree, so that, having died to sins,
   we might live for righteousness;
   by His wounding you have been healed.
For you were like sheep going astray,
   but you have now returned
   to the shepherd and guardian of your souls.

1 Peter 2:20b-25

Therefore since we also have such a large cloud of witnesses surrounding us, let us lay aside every weight and the sin that so easily ensnares us, and run with endurance the race that lies before us, keeping our eyes on Jesus, the source and perfecter of our faith, who for the joy that lay before Him endured a cross and despised the shame, and has sat down at the right hand of God's throne.

For consider Him who endured such hostility from sinners against Himself, so that you won't grow weary and lose heart.

Hebrews 12:1-3

Don't work for the food that perishes but for the food that lasts for eternal life, which the Son of Man will give you.

John 6:27a

We have confidence in the Lord about you, that you are doing and will do what we command. May the Lord direct your hearts to God's love and Christ's endurance.

2 Thessalonians 3:4-5

Growing Them in Character

There Are Reasons Behind the Rules

And now, Israel, what does the LORD your God ask of you except to fear the LORD your God by walking in all His ways, to love Him, and to serve the LORD your God with all your heart and all your soul, keeping the LORD's commandments and statutes that I am giving you today, for your own good?

Deuteronomy 10:12-13

Better the little that the righteous man has
    than the abundance of many wicked people.
For the arms of the wicked will be broken,
    but the LORD supports the righteous.
The LORD watches over
    the blameless all their days,
    and their inheritance will last forever.
They will not be disgraced in times of adversity;
    they will be satisfied in days of hunger.
But the wicked will perish;
    the LORD's enemies, like the glory
    of the pastures, will fade away—
    they will fade away like smoke.

Psalm 37:16-20

A little while, and the wicked will be no more;
    though you look for him, he will not be there.
But the humble will inherit the land
    and will enjoy abundant prosperity.

Psalm 37:10-11

Righteousness guards people of integrity,
    but wickedness undermines the sinner.

Proverbs 13:6

Blessed are those who
   hunger and thirst for righteousness,
   because they will be filled.
Blessed are the merciful,
   because they will be shown mercy.
Blessed are the pure in heart,
   because they will see God.
Blessed are the peacemakers,
   because they will be called sons of God.
Blessed are those who are
   persecuted for righteousness,
   because the kingdom of heaven is theirs.

Matthew 5:6-10

I have been young and now I am old,
   yet I have not seen the righteous abandoned
   or his children begging bread.
He is always generous, always lending,
   and his children are a blessing.

Psalm 37:25-26

Watch the blameless and observe the upright,
   for the man of peace will have a future.

Psalm 37:37

Do not let sin reign in your mortal body, so that you obey its desires. And do not offer any parts of it to sin as weapons for unrighteousness. But as those who are alive from the dead, offer yourselves to God, and all the parts of yourselves to God as weapons for righteousness. For sin will not rule over you, because you are not under law but under grace.

Romans 6:12-14

So great is my veneration for the Bible that the earlier my children begin to read it, the more confident will be my hope that they will prove useful citizens of their country and respectable members of society.

—John Quincy Adams

Thank God that, although you used to be slaves of sin, you obeyed from the heart that pattern of teaching you were entrusted to, and having been liberated from sin, you became enslaved to righteousness. . . .

For just as you offered the parts of yourselves as slaves to moral impurity, and to greater and greater lawlessness, so now offer them as slaves to righteousness, which results in sanctification.

For when you were slaves of sin, you were free from allegiance to righteousness. And what fruit was produced then from the things you are now ashamed of? For the end of those things is death.

But now, since you have been liberated from sin and become enslaved to God, you have your fruit, which results in sanctification—and the end is eternal life! For the wages of sin is death, but the gift of God is eternal life in Christ Jesus our Lord.

Romans 6:17-18, 20-23

Now you must also put away all the following: anger, wrath, malice, slander, and filthy language from your mouth. Do not lie to one another, since you have put off the old man with his practices and have put on the new man, who is being renewed in knowledge according to the image of his Creator.

Colossians 3:8-10

I have set before you life and death, blessing and curse. Choose life so that you and your descendants may live, loving the LORD your God, obeying Him, and clinging to Him. For He is your life.

Deuteronomy 30:19b-20a

Therefore, know that the LORD your God is God, the faithful God who keeps covenant loyalty to a thousandth generation for those who love Him and keep His commandments.

Deuteronomy 7:9

Training Them in Wisdom

Let's Learn What Really Matters

We are asking that you may be filled with the knowledge of His will in all wisdom and spiritual understanding, so that you may walk worthy of the Lord, fully pleasing to Him, bearing fruit in every good work and growing in the knowledge of God.

Colossians 1:9b-10

Now if any of you lacks wisdom, he should ask God, who gives to all generously and without criticizing, and it will be given to him.

But let him ask in faith without doubting. For the doubter is like the surging sea, driven and tossed by the wind. That person should not expect to receive anything from the Lord.

James 1:5-7

For I will give you such words and a wisdom that none of your adversaries will be able to resist or contradict.

Luke 21:15

But if you have bitter envy and selfish ambition in your heart, don't brag and lie in defiance of the truth. Such wisdom does not come down from above, but is earthly, sensual, demonic. For where envy and selfish ambition exist, there is disorder and every kind of evil.

But the wisdom from above is first pure, then peace-loving, gentle, compliant, full of mercy and good fruits.

James 3:14-17a

Promises to Get You Through

Accept my instruction instead of silver,
   and knowledge rather than pure gold.
For wisdom is better than precious stones,
   and nothing desirable can compare with it.
I, Wisdom, share a home with shrewdness
   and have knowledge and discretion. . . .
I possess good advice and competence;
   I have understanding and strength.
It is by me that kings reign
   and rulers enact just law;
   by me, princes lead,
   as do nobles and all righteous judges.
I love those who love me,
   and those who search for me find me.
With me are riches and honor,
   lasting wealth and righteousness.
My fruit is better than solid gold,
   and my harvest than pure silver.
I walk in the way of righteousness,
   along the paths of justice,
   giving wealth as an inheritance
   to those who love me,
   and filling their treasuries.

Proverbs 8:10-12, 14-21

And now, my sons, listen to me;
   those who keep my ways are happy.
Listen to instruction and be wise;
   don't ignore it.
Anyone who listens to me is happy,
   watching at my doors every day,
   waiting by the posts of my doorway.
For the one who finds me finds life
   and obtains favor from the LORD.

Proverbs 8:32-35

*We count the Scriptures of God to be
the most sublime philosophy. I find
more marks of authenticity in the
Bible than in any profane history
whatsoever!*

–Isaac Newton

My son, if you accept my words
  and store up my commands within you,
  listening closely to wisdom
  and directing your heart to understanding;
  furthermore, if you call out to insight
  and lift your voice to understanding,
  if you seek it like silver and
  search for it like hidden treasure,
  then you will understand the fear of the LORD
  and discover the knowledge of God. . . .
Then you will understand righteousness, justice,
  and integrity—every good path.
For wisdom will enter your heart,
  and knowledge will delight your soul.
Discretion will watch over you,
  and understanding will guard you,
  rescuing you from the way of evil.

Proverbs 2:1-5, 9-12a

The fear of the LORD
   is the beginning of wisdom;
   all who follow His instructions
   have good insight.

Psalm 111:10a

The fear of the LORD is wisdom's instruction,
   and humility comes before honor.

Proverbs 15:33

Hold on to instruction; don't let go.
   Guard it, for it is your life.

Proverbs 4:13

This also comes from the LORD of Hosts.
   He gives wonderful advice;
   He gives great wisdom.

Isaiah 28:29

I will sing about the LORD's faithful love
   forever; with my mouth I will proclaim
   Your faithfulness to all generations.

Psalm 89:1

Correcting Them in Love

I'm Just Doing What's Best for You

No discipline seems enjoyable at the time, but painful. Later on, however, it yields the fruit of peace and righteousness to those who have been trained by it.

Hebrews 12:11

My son, do not take the Lord's discipline lightly, or faint when you are reproved by Him; for the Lord disciplines the one He loves, and punishes every son whom He receives.

Hebrews 12:5b-6

Do you actually think that I take pleasure in the death of the wicked, declares the Lord GOD, and not rather that he should turn from his ways, and live?

Ezekiel 18:23

Anyone who ignores instruction
   despises himself,
   but whoever listens to correction
   acquires good sense.

Proverbs 15:32

Poverty and disgrace come
   to those who ignore instruction,
   but the one who accepts rebuke
   will be honored.

Proverbs 13:18

This is love: that we walk according to His commands. This is the command as you have heard it from the beginning: you must walk in love.

2 John 6

Do you not know that if you offer yourselves to someone as obedient slaves, you are slaves of that one you obey—either of sin leading to death or of obedience leading to righteousness?

Romans 6:16

But encourage each other daily, while it is still called today, so that none of you is hardened by sin's deception. For we have become companions of the Messiah if we hold firmly until the end the reality that we had at the start.

Hebrews 3:13-14

Blessed is a man who endures trials, because when he passes the test he will receive the crown of life He has promised to those who love Him.

James 1:12

Correcting Them in Love

All Scripture is inspired by God and is profitable for teaching, for rebuking, for correcting, for training in righteousness.

2 Timothy 3:16

When you walk here and there,
　they will guide you;
　when you lie down, they will watch over you;
　when you wake up, they will talk to you.
For a command is a lamp, teaching is a light,
　and corrective instructions are the way to life.

Proverbs 6:22-23

A Bible and a newspaper in every house and a good school in every district are the principal support of virtue, morality, and civil liberty.
—Ben Franklin

I have clearly heard Ephraim moaning:
"You disciplined me,
   and I have become disciplined
   like an untrained calf!
Restore me, that I may return,
   for you, O LORD, are my God.
After I turned aside, I repented.
   After I was instructed, I showed remorse.
I was ashamed and humiliated,
   because I carried the disgrace
   of my youthful follies."
Ephraim is indeed a precious son to Me,
   a favored child.
For though I speak against him so often,
   I do certainly bring him back to mind.
Therefore, My inner being yearns for him;
   I will truly have compassion on him,
   says the LORD.

Jeremiah 31:18-20

Correcting Them in Love

He personally gave some to be . . . teachers, for the training of the saints in the work of ministry, to build up the body of Christ, until we all reach unity in the faith and in the knowledge of God's Son, growing into a mature man with a stature measured by Christ's fullness.

Then we will no longer be little children, tossed by the waves and blown around by every wind of teaching, by human cunning with cleverness in the techniques of deceit. But speaking the truth in love, let us grow in every way into Him who is the head—Christ. From Him the whole body, fitted and knit together by every supporting ligament, promotes the growth of the body for building up itself in love by the proper working of each individual part.

Ephesians 4:11-16

See! Blessed is the man whom God corrects;
  do not reject the discipline of the Almighty.
For He crushes, but He also binds up;
  He strikes, but His hands also heal.

Job 5:17-18

Igniting Them to Excellence

Your Best Is Not Too Much to Ask

Do everything without grumbling and arguing, so that you may be blameless and pure, children of God who are faultless in a crooked and perverted generation, among whom you shine like stars in the world. Hold firmly the message of life. Then I can boast in the day of Christ that I didn't run in vain or labor for nothing.

Philippians 2:14-16

Now if Christ is in you, the body is dead because of sin, but the Spirit is life because of righteousness. And if the Spirit of Him who raised Jesus from the dead lives in you, then He who raised Christ from the dead will also bring your mortal bodies to life through His Spirit who lives in you.

Romans 8:10-11

Walk by the Spirit and you will not carry out the desire of the flesh. For the flesh desires what is against the Spirit, and the Spirit desires what is against the flesh; these are opposed to each other, so that you don't do what you want.

Galatians 5:16-17

Therefore, brothers, by the mercies of God, I urge you to present your bodies as a living sacrifice, holy and pleasing to God; this is your spiritual worship. Do not be conformed to this age, but be transformed by the renewing of your mind, so that you may discern what is the good, pleasing, and perfect will of God.

Romans 12:1-2

Finally then, brothers, we ask and encourage you in the Lord Jesus, that as you have received from us how you must walk and please God— as you are doing—do so even more. For you know what commands we gave you through the Lord Jesus.

1 Thessalonians 4:1-2

Based on the gift they have received, everyone should use it to serve others, as good managers of the varied grace of God. If anyone speaks, his speech should be like the oracles of God; if anyone serves, his service should be from the strength God provides, so that in every-thing God may be glorified through Jesus Christ. To Him belong the glory and the power forever and ever. Amen.

1 Peter 4:10-11

Do not lack diligence; be fervent in spirit; serve the Lord.

Romans 12:11

For you are called to freedom, brothers;
only don't use this freedom as an opportunity
for the flesh, but serve one another through love.
For the entire law is fulfilled in one statement:
"You shall love your neighbor as yourself."

Galatians 5:13-14

Practice these things; be committed to them,
so that your progress may be evident to all.

1 Timothy 4:15

*Scripture is the school of the Holy
Spirit, in which, as nothing is omit-
ted that is both necessary and useful
to know, so nothing is taught but
what is expedient to know.*

—John Calvin

My son, pay attention to my words;
   listen closely to my sayings.
Don't lose sight of them;
   keep them within your heart.
For they are life to those who find them,
   and health to one's whole body.
Guard your heart above all else,
   for it is the source of life.
Don't let your mouth speak dishonestly,
   and don't let your lips talk deviously.
Let your eyes look forward;
   fix your gaze straight ahead.
Carefully consider the path for your feet,
   and all your ways will be established.
Don't turn to the right or to the left;
   keep your feet away from evil.

Proverbs 4:20-27

Igniting Them to Excellence

Your eyes will see your Teacher, and whenever you turn to the right or to the left, your ears will hear this command behind you: "This is the way. Walk in it."

Isaiah 30:20b-21

I labor for this, striving with His strength that works powerfully in me.

Colossians 1:29

And I will show you an even better way.

1 Corinthians 12:31b

The plans of the diligent
    certainly lead to profit,
    but anyone who is reckless
    only becomes poor.

Proverbs 21:5

The slacker craves, yet has nothing,
    but the diligent is fully satisfied.

Proverbs 13:4

Promises for Nights and Weekends

Not every day is a school day. Not every waking hour is earmarked for work.

You're a teacher, yes. But you're much more than a teacher. Perhaps you have a family to take care of. Perhaps other interest areas occupy a good deal of your time, keeping you busy at church, in clubs and organizations, and around your community.

So . . . what does God want you doing when you're not doing your teaching? More importantly, who does God want you being when you're just being yourself?

Making Time to Rest

I Can't Run This Hard All the Time

The LORD is good
  to those who hope in Him—
  to the one who seeks Him.
It is good for one to wait silently
  for the LORD's salvation.

Lamentations 3:25-26

I am faint and severely crushed;
  I groan because of the anguish of my heart.
Lord, my every desire is known to You;
  my sighing is not hidden from You.
My heart races, my strength leaves me,
  and even the light of my eyes has faded.

Psalm 38:8-10

I said, "If only I had wings like a dove!
  I would fly away and find rest.
How far away I would flee;
  I would stay in the wilderness.
I would hurry to my shelter
  from the raging wind and the storm."

Psalm 55:6-8

The spirit is willing, but the flesh is weak.

Matthew 26:41b

If I say, "My foot is slipping,"
  Your faithful love will support me, LORD.
When I am filled with cares,
  Your comfort brings me joy.

Psalm 94:18-19

I keep the Lord in mind always.
  Because He is at my right hand,
  I will not be defeated.
Therefore my heart is glad, and my spirit
  rejoices; my body also rests securely.
For You will not abandon me to Sheol;
  You will not allow Your Faithful One
  to see the Pit.
You reveal the path of life to me;
  in Your presence is abundant joy;
  in Your right hand are eternal pleasures.

Psalm 16:8-11

You will keep in perfect peace
  the mind that is dependent on You,
  for it is trusting in You.

Isaiah 26:3

Return to your rest, my soul,
  for the LORD has been good to you.
For You, LORD, rescued me from death,
  my eyes from tears,
  my feet from stumbling.

Psalm 116:7-8

Therefore strengthen your tired hands and weakened knees, and make straight paths for your feet, so that what is lame may not be dislocated, but healed instead.

Hebrews 12:12-13

Cast your burden on the LORD,
  and He will support you;
He will never allow
  the righteous to be shaken.

Psalm 55:22

Every hour I read you kills a sin / Or lets a virtue in / To fight against it.
—Izaak Walton

The LORD is my shepherd;
  there is nothing I lack.
He lets me lie down in green pastures;
  He leads me beside quiet waters.
He renews my life; He leads me
  along the right paths for His name's sake.
Even when I go through the darkest valley,
  I am not afraid of any danger,
  for You are with me;
  Your rod and Your staff—
  they give me comfort.
You prepare a table before me
  in full view of my enemies;
  You anoint my head with oil;
  my cup is full.
Only goodness and faithful love
  will pursue me all the days of my life,
  and I will dwell in the house of the LORD
  as long as I live.

Psalm 23:1-6

Making Time to Rest

I know nothing is better for anyone than to
rejoice and to accomplish good with their lives.
Also, it is God's gift whenever anyone eats,
drinks, and experiences good in all his struggle.
Ecclesiastes 3:12-13

The sleep of the worker is sweet.
Ecclesiastes 5:12a

The Lord GOD, the Holy One of Israel,
has said: "You will be delivered by returning
and resting; your strength will lie in quiet
confidence."
Isaiah 30:15a

The result of righteousness will be peace;
   the effect of righteousness
   will be quiet confidence forever.
Then My people will dwell
   in a peaceful place,
   and in safe and restful dwellings.
Isaiah 32:17-18

Focusing on Your Family

I'm the Only One of Me That They Have

Go around Zion,
   encircle it; count its towers,
   note its ramparts; tour its citadels
   so that you can tell a future generation:
"This God, our God forever and ever—
   He will lead us eternally."

Psalm 48:12-14

Take note of all these words I am declaring
as a testimony against you this day, so that you
may command your children to be careful to
follow all the words of this law. For it is not a
word that has no meaning for you; rather it is
your life.

Deuteronomy 32:46-47a

Only take care and diligently watch yourselves so you don't forget the things your eyes
have seen, so they don't slip from your mind
all the days of your life. Teach them to your
children and your grandchildren.

Deuteronomy 4:9

Tell your children about it,
    and let your children tell their children,
    and their children the next generation.

Joel 1:3

Teach a youth about the way he should go;
    even when he is old
    he will not depart from it.

Proverbs 22:6

See that you don't look down on one of these little ones, because I tell you that in heaven their angels continually view the face of My Father in heaven. For the Son of Man has come to save the lost.

What do you think? If a man has 100 sheep, and one of them goes astray, won't he leave the 99 on the hillside, and go and search for the stray? And if he finds it, I assure you: He rejoices over that sheep more than over the 99 that did not go astray.

In the same way, it is not the will of your Father in heaven that one of these little ones perish.

Matthew 18:10-14

Then He took a child, had him stand among them, and taking him in His arms, He said to them, "Whoever welcomes one little child such as this in My name welcomes Me. And whoever welcomes Me does not welcome Me, but Him who sent Me."

Mark 9:36-37

I am not seeking what is yours, but you. For children are not obligated to save up for their parents, but parents for their children. I will most gladly spend and be spent for you.

2 Corinthians 12:14b-15a

My eyes favor the faithful of the land
  so that they may sit down with me.
The one who follows
  the way of integrity may serve me.

Psalm 101:6

*What is a home without a Bible? /
'Tis a home where daily bread / For
the body is provided / But the soul
is never fed.*

—Charles D. Meigs

I will declare wise sayings;
I will speak mysteries from the past—
things we have heard and known
and that our fathers have passed down to us.
We must not hide them from their children,
but must tell a future generation
the praises of the LORD, His might,
and the wonderful works He has performed.
He established a testimony in Jacob
and set up a law in Israel,
which He commanded our fathers
to teach to their children
so that a future generation—
children yet to be born—might know.
They were to rise and tell their children
so that they might put
their confidence in God
and not forget God's works,
but keep His commandments.

Psalm 78:2-7

Do not exasperate your children, so they won't become discouraged.

Colossians 3:21

Be conscientious about yourself and your teaching; persevere in these things, for by doing so you will save both yourself and your hearers.

1 Timothy 4:16

And I pray this: that your love will keep on growing in knowledge and every kind of discernment, so that you can determine what really matters and can be pure and blameless in the day of Christ, filled with the fruit of right-eousness that comes through Jesus Christ, to the glory and praise of God.

Philippians 1:9-11

Let the message about the Messiah dwell richly among you, teaching and admonishing one another in all wisdom, and singing psalms, hymns, and spiritual songs, with gratitude in your hearts to God.

Colossians 3:16

Striking a Balance

I Know I Can't Do Everything

Whom do I have in heaven but You?
  And I desire nothing on earth but You.
My flesh and my heart may fail,
  but God is the strength of my heart,
  my portion forever.

Psalm 73:25-26

We have this kind of confidence toward God through Christ: not that we are competent in ourselves to consider anything as coming from ourselves, but our competence is from God.

2 Corinthians 3:4-5

This is why I tell you: Don't worry about your life, what you will eat or what you will drink; or about your body, what you will wear.

Isn't life more than food and the body more than clothing?

Look at the birds of the sky: they don't sow or reap or gather into barns, yet your heavenly Father feeds them. Aren't you worth more than they? Can any of you add a single cubit to his height by worrying?

Matthew 6:25-27

A man's steps are established by the LORD,
  and He takes pleasure in his way.
Though he falls, he will not be overwhelmed,
  because the LORD holds his hand.

Psalm 37:23-24

The LORD is good,
  a stronghold in a day of distress;
He cares for those who take refuge in Him.
Nahum 1:7

And if you address as Father the One who judges impartially based on each one's work, you are to conduct yourselves in reverence during this time of temporary residence.
  For you know that you were redeemed from your empty way of life inherited from the fathers, not with perishable things, like silver or gold, but with the precious blood of Christ.
1 Peter 1:17-19a

Therefore, whether you eat or drink, or whatever you do, do everything for God's glory.
1 Corinthians 10:31

Do not grow weary in doing good.
2 Thessalonians 3:13

Don't worry about anything, but in everything, through prayer and petition with thanksgiving, let your requests be made known to God. And the peace of God, which surpasses every thought, will guard your hearts and your minds in Christ Jesus.

Philippians 4:6-7

And whatever you do, in word or in deed, do everything in the name of the Lord Jesus.

Colossians 3:17a

'Thinking Christianly' is thinking by Christians about anything and everything in a consistently Christian way— in a manner that is shaped, directed, and restrained by the truth of God's Word and God's Spirit.

—Os Guiness

Everything has its appointed hour,
every matter its time under the heavens:
a time to give birth and a time to die;
a time to plant
and a time to uproot what is planted;
a time to kill and a time to heal;
a time to tear down and a time to build up;
a time to weep and a time to laugh;
a time to mourn and a time to dance;
a time to throw stones away
and a time to gather stones;
a time to embrace and a time
to keep one's distance from embracing;
a time to search and a time to count as lost;
a time to keep and a time to throw away;
a time to tear and a time to sew;
a time to be silent and a time to speak;
a time to love and a time to hate;
a time for war and a time for peace.

Ecclesiastes 3:1-8

Striking a Balance

Now the end of all things is near; therefore, be clear-headed and disciplined for prayer. Above all, keep your love for one another at full strength, since love covers a multitude of sins.

1 Peter 4:7-8

Be in agreement with one another. Do not be proud; instead, associate with the humble. Do not be wise in your own estimation. Do not repay anyone evil for evil. Try to do what is honorable in everyone's eyes. If possible, on your part, live at peace with everyone.

Romans 12:16-18

If anyone considers himself to be something when he is nothing, he is deceiving himself.

Galatians 6:3

But the fruit of the Spirit is love, joy, peace, patience, kindness, goodness, faith, gentleness, self-control. Against such things there is no law.

Galatians 5:22-23

Keeping it Simple

Should Life Really Be This Complicated?

Seek to lead a quiet life, to mind your own business, and to work with your own hands, as we commanded you, so that you may walk properly in the presence of outsiders and not be dependent on anyone.

1 Thessalonians 4:11-12

Come, let us worship and bow down;
    let us kneel before the LORD our Maker.
For He is our God,
    and we are the people of His pasture,
    the sheep under His care.

Psalm 95:6-7

He will stand and shepherd them
    in the strength of the LORD,
    in the majestic name of the LORD His God.
They will live securely,
    for at that time His greatness
    will extend to the ends of the earth.
This One will be the source of peace.

Micah 5:4-5a

Our mouths were filled with laughter then,
    and our tongues with shouts of joy.
Then they said among the nations,
    "The LORD has done great things for them."
The LORD had done great things for us;
    we were joyful.

Psalm 126:2-3

You are the light of the world. A city situated on a hill cannot be hidden.

No one lights a lamp and puts it under a basket, but rather on a lampstand, and it gives light for all who are in the house.

In the same way, let your light shine before men, so that they may see your good works and give glory to your Father in heaven.

Matthew 5:14-16

I want you to insist on these things, so that those who have believed God might be careful to devote themselves to good works. These are good and profitable for everyone.

Titus 3:8b

Pure and undefiled religion before our God and Father is this: to look after orphans and widows in their distress and to keep oneself unstained by the world.

James 1:27

Come to Me, all you who are weary and burdened, and I will give you rest.

Take My yoke upon you and learn from Me, because I am gentle and humble in heart, and you will find rest for your souls.

Matthew 11:28-29

A Sabbath rest remains, therefore, for God's people. For the person who has entered His rest has rested from his own works, just as God did from His.

Hebrews 4:9-10

Calmness puts great sins to rest.

Ecclesiastes 10:4b

Bible reading is an education in itself.
—Lord Tennyson

Trust in the LORD and do good;
   dwell in the land and live securely.
Take delight in the LORD,
   and He will give you your heart's desires.
Commit your way to the LORD;
   trust in Him, and He will act,
   making your righteousness
   shine like the dawn,
   your justice like the noonday.
Be silent before the LORD
   and wait expectantly for Him;
   do not be agitated by one
   who prospers in his way,
   by the man who
   carries out evil plans.

Psalm 37:3-7

Peace I leave with you. My peace I give to
you. I do not give to you as the world gives.
Your heart must not be troubled or fearful.

John 14:27

Therefore if the Son sets you free, you really
will be free.

John 8:36

LORD, You are my portion and my
   cup of blessing; You hold my future.
The boundary lines have
   fallen for me in pleasant places;
   indeed, I have a beautiful inheritance.

Psalm 16:5-6

LORD, my heart is not proud;
   my eyes are not haughty.
I do not get involved with things
   too great or too difficult for me.
Instead, I have calmed and quieted myself
   like a little weaned child with its mother;
   I am like a little child.

Psalm 131:1-2

Promises
for
All You Are

Teaching may be your profession, but the discovery of truth is your life. Math or history may be your subjects of choice, but the Bible is your textbook of record. The classroom may be your field of operations, but the prayer closet is your proving ground.

All these things unite to form the person you are, to fulfill the calling of God on your life. It's not an easy walk, but it's the only one worth traveling. It's not a pathway to riches but a true investment in people's lives. It's not a thrill a minute but the promise of an eternal purpose.

A Taste for Learning

Lord, Keep Me Hungry, Keep Me Growing

The LORD's works are great,
  studied by all who delight in them.
All that He does is splendid and majestic;
  His righteousness endures forever.
He has caused His wonderful works
  to be remembered.

Psalm 111:2-4a

LORD, I have heard the report about You;
  I stand in awe, O LORD, of Your deeds.

Habakkuk 3:2a

I remember the days of old;
  I meditate on all You have done;
  I reflect on the work of Your hands.

Psalm 143:5

For His divine power has given us everything
required for life and godliness, through the
knowledge of Him who called us by His own
glory and goodness. By these He has given
us very great and precious promises, so that
through them you may share in the divine
nature, escaping the corruption that is in
the world because of evil desires.

2 Peter 1:3-4

In Him all the treasures
  of wisdom and knowledge are hidden.

Colossians 2:3

Promises for All You Are

A house is built by wisdom,
  and it is established by understanding;
  by knowledge the rooms are filled
  with every precious and beautiful treasure.
                                              Proverbs 24:3-4

There is gold and a multitude of jewels,
  but knowledgeable lips are a rare treasure.
                                              Proverbs 20:15

Oh, the depth of the riches
  both of the wisdom
  and the knowledge of God!
How unsearchable His judgments
  and untraceable His ways!
For who has known the mind of the Lord?
  Or who has been His counselor?
Or who has ever first given to Him,
  and has to be repaid?
For from Him and through Him
  and to Him are all things.
                                              Romans 11:33-36a

A Taste for Learning

May the name of God
  be praised forever and ever,
  for wisdom and power belong to Him.
He changes the times and seasons;
  He removes kings and establishes kings.
He gives wisdom to the wise
  and knowledge to those
  who have understanding.
He reveals the deep and hidden things;
  He knows what is in the darkness,
  and light dwells with Him.

Daniel 2:20b-22

*In any complete revelation of God's
mind, will, character, and being, there
must be things hard for the beginner
to understand; and the wisest and
best of us are but beginners.*

–R. A. Torrey

O LORD, our Lord, how magnificent
  is Your name throughout the earth!
You have covered the heavens
  with Your majesty. . . .
When I observe Your heavens,
  the work of Your fingers,
  the moon and the stars,
  which You set in place,
  what is man, that You remember him,
  the son of man, that You look after him?
You made him little less than God
  and crowned him with glory and honor.
You made him lord
  over the works of Your hands;
  You put everything under his feet. . . .
O LORD, our Lord, how magnificent
  is Your name throughout the earth!

Psalm 8:1, 3-6, 9

A Taste for Learning

Instruct a wise man,
and he will be wiser still;
teach a righteous man,
and he will learn more.

Proverbs 9:9

A wise man will listen
and increase his learning,
and a discerning man will obtain guidance.

Proverbs 1:5

Guard what has been entrusted to you, avoiding irreverent, empty speech and contradictions from the "knowledge" that falsely bears that name. By professing it, some people have deviated from the faith.

1 Timothy 6:20-21a

But grow in the grace and knowledge of our Lord and Savior Jesus Christ. To Him be the glory both now and to the day of eternity.

2 Peter 3:18

A Feel
for Perspective

Help Me Not to Get Bent out of Shape

Proclaim the message; persist in it whether convenient or not; rebuke, correct, and encourage with great patience and teaching.

2 Timothy 4:2

This saying is trustworthy and deserving of full acceptance: "Christ Jesus came into the world to save sinners"—and I am the worst of them.

But I received mercy because of this, so that in me, the worst of them, Christ Jesus might demonstrate the utmost patience as an example to those who would believe in Him for eternal life.

1 Timothy 1:15-16

Now we want each of you to demonstrate the same diligence for the final realization of your hope, so that you won't become lazy, but imitators of those who inherit the promises through faith and perseverance.

Hebrews 6:11-12

For God is not unjust; He will not forget your work and the love you showed for His name when you served the saints—and you continue to serve them.

Hebrews 6:10

This is what the LORD says,
  "Stand by the roadways and look.
Ask about the ancient paths,
  where the good way is,
    then walk on it and find rest for yourselves."
Jeremiah 6:16a

Therefore, brothers, be patient until the
Lord's coming. See how the farmer waits for
the precious fruit of the earth and is patient
with it until it receives the early and the late
rains. You also must be patient. Strengthen
your hearts, because the Lord's coming is near.
James 5:7-8

And we exhort you, brothers: warn those
who are lazy, comfort the discouraged, help
the weak, be patient with everyone. See to it
that no one repays evil for evil to anyone, but
always pursue what is good for one another
and for all.

1 Thessalonians 5:14-15

Rejoice in hope; be patient in affliction; be persistent in prayer. Share with the saints in their needs; pursue hospitality.

Bless those who persecute you; bless and do not curse. Rejoice with those who rejoice; weep with those who weep.

Romans 12:12-15

A person's insight gives him patience,
and his virtue is to overlook an offense.

Proverbs 19:11

You may never have all your difficulties solved or all your objections met, but you can be sure of your foundation. You can feel that your feet are planted in the Rock of Ages.

–Addison Howard Gibson

As God's ministers, we commend ourselves:
  by great endurance, by afflictions,
  by hardship, by pressures . . .
  by sleepless nights, by times of hunger,
  by purity, by knowledge,
  by patience, by kindness,
  by the Holy Spirit, by sincere love,
  by the message of truth, by the power of God;
  through weapons of righteousness
    on the right hand and the left,
  through glory and dishonor,
    through slander and good report;
  as deceivers yet true;
  as unknown yet recognized;
  as dying and look—we live;
  as being chastened yet not killed;
  as grieving yet always rejoicing;
  as poor yet enriching many;
  as having nothing yet possessing everything.

2 Corinthians 6:4b, 5b-10

A Feel for Perspective

With what should I come before the LORD,
  and bow myself before God on high?
Should I come before Him
  with burnt offerings, with year-old calves?
Would the LORD be pleased
  with thousands of rams,
  with streams of oil by the ten thousands?
Should I give my firstborn for my transgression,
  the fruit of my body for my own sin?
  He has told you, O man, what is good.
And what does the LORD require of you
  other than to act justly, to love faithfulness,
  and to walk carefully with your God?

Micah 6:6-8

Until I expire, I will not give up my integrity.
  I will cling to my righteousness
  and never let go.

Job 27:5b-6a

For He Himself has said, "I will never leave
you or forsake you."

Hebrews 13:5b

A Voice of Encouragement

Tell Me, Lord, That I Can Do This

Look! You have instructed many
and strengthened weak hands.
Your words have steadied the one who stumbles;
you have strengthened faltering knees.

Job 4:3-4

Do not fear, for I am with you;
  do not be afraid, for I am your God.
I will strengthen you; I will help you;
  I will support you with
  My righteous right hand.

Isaiah 41:10

Call on Me in a day of trouble;
  I will rescue you, and you will honor Me.

Psalm 50:15

For You are my hope, Lord GOD,
  my confidence from my youth.
I have leaned on You from birth;
  You took me from my mother's womb.
My praise is always about You.

Psalm 71:5-6

The name of the LORD is a strong tower;
  the righteous run to it and are protected.

Proverbs 18:10

Everything, dear friends,
  is for building you up.

2 Corinthians 12:19b

For all of them were trying to intimidate us,
saying, "They will become discouraged in the
work, and it will never be finished." But now,
my God, strengthen my hands.

Nehemiah 6:9

I love You, LORD, my strength.

Psalm 18:1

I am able to do all things through Him who
strengthens me.

Philippians 4:13

And may the Lord cause you to increase and
overflow with love for one another and for
everyone, just as we also do for you.

1 Thessalonians 3:12

A Voice of Encouragement

I waited patiently for the LORD,
   and He turned to me
   and heard my cry for help. . . .
He put a new song in my mouth,
   a hymn of praise to our God.
Many will see and fear,
   and put their trust in the LORD.

Psalm 40:1, 3

May the God of hope fill you with all joy and peace in believing, so that you may overflow with hope by the power of the Holy Spirit.

Romans 15:13

The Scripture says that in His own sweet way / If we but wait / The Lord will take our burdens and set crooked matters straight.

—John Henry Jowett

Promises for All You Are

I raise my eyes toward the mountains.
  Where will my help come from?
My help comes from the LORD,
  the Maker of heaven and earth.
He will not allow your foot to slip;
  your Protector will not slumber.
Indeed, the Protector of Israel
  does not slumber or sleep.
The LORD protects you;
  the LORD is a shelter right by your side.
The sun will not strike you by day,
  or the moon by night.
The LORD will protect you from all harm;
  He will protect your life.
The LORD will protect your coming and going
  both now and forever.

Psalm 121:1-8

Give thanks in everything, for this is God's will for you in Christ Jesus.

1 Thessalonians 5:18

Rest in God alone, my soul,
  for my hope comes from Him.
He alone is my rock and my salvation,
  my stronghold; I will not be shaken.
My salvation and glory depend on God;
  my strong rock, my refuge, is in God.

Psalm 62:5-7

So don't throw away your confidence, which has a great reward. For you need endurance, so that after you have done God's will, you may receive what was promised.

For in yet a very little while, the Coming One will come and not delay. But My righteous one will live by faith; and if he draws back, My soul has no pleasure in him. But we are not those who draw back and are destroyed, but those who have faith and obtain life.

Hebrews 10:35-39

An Ear *for* God's Word

I Want the Bible to Be an Open Book

I will meditate on Your precepts
  and think about Your ways. . . .
Your statutes are the theme of my song
  during my earthly life.
I remember Your name in the night, LORD,
  and I keep Your law.
This is my practice:
  I obey Your precepts.

Psalm 119:15, 54-56

How happy are those whose way is blameless,
    who live according to the law of the LORD!
Happy are those who keep His decrees
    and seek Him with all their heart.

Psalm 119:1-2

Instruction from Your lips is better for me
    than thousands of gold and silver pieces.

Psalm 119:72

Your decrees are my delight and my counselors.

Psalm 119:24

Every word of God is pure;
    He is a shield to those
    who take refuge in Him.

Proverbs 30:5

For whatever was written before was
written for our instruction, so that through
our endurance and through the encouragement
of the Scriptures we may have hope.

Romans 15:4

Evil people and imposters will become worse, deceiving and being deceived.

But as for you, continue in what you have learned and firmly believed, knowing those from whom you learned, and that from childhood you have known the sacred Scriptures, which are able to instruct you for salvation through faith in Christ Jesus.

2 Timothy 3:13-15

The wise will be put to shame;
   they will be dismayed and snared.
They have rejected the word of the LORD,
   so what wisdom do they really have?

Jeremiah 8:9

I have Your decrees as a heritage forever;
   indeed, they are the joy of my heart.
I am resolved to obey Your statutes
   to the very end.

Psalm 119:111-112

The instruction of the LORD
  is perfect, reviving the soul;
  the testimony of the LORD is trustworthy,
  making the inexperienced wise.
The precepts of the LORD are right,
  making the heart glad;
  the commandment of the LORD is radiant,
  making the eyes light up.

Psalm 19:7-8

Sink the Bible to the bottom of the ocean, and still man's obligations to God would be unchanged. He would have the same path to tread, only his lamp and guide would be gone; the same voyage to make, but his chart and compass would be overboard.

—Henry Ward Beecher

LORD, Your word is forever;
   it is firmly fixed in heaven.
Your faithfulness is for all generations;
   You established the earth,
   and it stands firm.
They stand today in accordance
   with Your judgments,
   for all things are Your servants.
If Your instruction had not been my delight,
   I would have died in my affliction.
I will never forget Your precepts,
   for You have given me
   life through them. . . .
I have seen a limit to all perfection,
   but Your command is without limit.
How I love Your teaching!
   It is my meditation all day long.

                    Psalm 119:89-93, 96-97

An Ear for God's Word

Open my eyes so that I may see
wonderful things in Your law.

Psalm 119:18

For the word of God is living and effective
and sharper than any two-edged sword, pene-
trating as far as to divide soul, spirit, joints,
and marrow; it is a judge of the ideas and
thoughts of the heart.

Hebrews 4:12

Your word is a lamp for my feet
and a light on my path.

Psalm 119:105

In addition, Your servant is warned by them;
there is great reward in keeping them.

Psalm 19:11

Remember Your word to Your servant,
through which You have given me hope.
This is my comfort in my affliction:
Your promise has given me life.

Psalm 119:49-50

An Eye on Eternity

Help Me Stay Focused on Forever

Lord, You have been our refuge
in every generation.
Before the mountains were born,
before You gave birth
to the earth and the world,
from eternity to eternity, You are God.

Psalm 90:1-2

O God, You are my God;
    I eagerly seek You.
My soul thirsts for You;
    my body faints for You in a land
    that is dry, desolate, and without water.
So I gaze on You in the sanctuary
    to see Your strength and Your glory.

Psalm 63:1-2

I have asked one thing from the LORD;
    it is what I desire:
    to dwell in the house of the LORD
    all the days of my life,
    gazing on the beauty of the LORD
    and seeking Him in His temple.

Psalm 27:4

For here we do not have an enduring city;
instead, we seek the one to come. Therefore,
through Him let us continually offer up to
God a sacrifice of praise, that is, the fruit of
our lips that confess His name.

Hebrews 13:14-15

I have often told you, and now say again with tears, that many live as enemies of the cross of Christ. Their end is destruction; their god is their stomach; their glory is in their shame.

They are focused on earthly things, but our citizenship is in heaven, from which we also eagerly wait for a Savior, the Lord Jesus Christ.

He will transform the body of our humble condition into the likeness of His glorious body, by the power that enables Him to subject everything to Himself.

Philippians 3:18-21

So if you have been raised with the Messiah, seek what is above, where the Messiah is, seated at the right hand of God. Set your minds on what is above, not on what is on the earth.

For you have died, and your life is hidden with the Messiah in God. When the Messiah, who is your life, is revealed, then you also will be revealed with Him in glory.

Colossians 3:1-4

Therefore we do not give up; even though our outer person is being destroyed, our inner person is being renewed day by day. For our momentary light affliction is producing for us an absolutely incomparable eternal weight of glory. So we do not focus on what is seen, but on what is unseen; for what is seen is temporary, but what is unseen is eternal.

2 Corinthians 4:16-18

As there is but one sun to enlighten the world naturally, so there is but one book to enlighten the world spiritually. May that Book become to each of us the guide of our journey, the inspiration of our thought, and our support and comfort in life and in death.

–Andrew Galloway

Then he showed me the river of living water, sparkling like crystal, flowing from the throne of God and of the Lamb down the middle of the broad street of the city.

On both sides of the river was the tree of life bearing 12 kinds of fruit, producing its fruit every month. The leaves of the tree are for healing the nations, and there will no longer be any curse.

The throne of God and of the Lamb will be in the city, and His servants will serve Him.

They will see His face, and His name will be on their foreheads. Night will no longer exist, and people will not need lamplight or sunlight, because the Lord God will give them light.

And they will reign forever and ever.

Revelation 22:1-5

The righteous thrive like a palm tree
   and grow like a cedar tree in Lebanon.
Planted in the house of the LORD,
   they thrive in the courtyards of our God.
They will still bear fruit in old age,
   healthy and green, to declare:
   "The LORD is just;
   He is my rock, and there is
   no unrighteousness in Him."

Psalm 92:12-15

How happy is everyone
   who fears the LORD,
   who walks in His ways!
You will surely eat
   what your hands have worked for.
You will be happy,
   and it will go well for you.

Psalm 128:1-2

And when the chief Shepherd appears, you
will receive the unfading crown of glory.

1 Peter 5:4

*Look for these other Bible Promise books
to give to the special people in your life.*

Bible Promises for Mom
0-8054-2732-5

Bible Promises for Dad
0-8054-2733-3

**Bible Promises for
the Graduate**
0-8054-2741-4

**Bible Promises for
My Teacher**
0-8054-2734-1

Available in August 2003
Bible Promises for Kids 0-8054-2740-6
Bible Promises for Teens 0-8054-2739-2
Bible Promises for New Believers 0-8054-2742-2
Bible Promises for New Parents 0-8054-2738-4